Grolier's
HOW TO STUDY
Course

Write
Papers

By
Ron Fry

 Grolier Educational Corporation
SHERMAN TURNPIKE, DANBURY, CONNECTICUT 06816

Grolier's **HOW TO STUDY** *Course:* **Write Papers**
ISBN 0-7172-7171-4

Cover design by Dean Johnson Design, Inc.

Printed in the United States of America

Table of Contents

Write Papers

Introduction

Taming The Dreaded "R" Monster

It's going to happen.

There you'll be, sitting quietly in class, contemplating the weekend to come, minding your own business.

Suddenly, without even a warning, your teacher will announce that your next assignment is...to write a Research Paper.

There's no getting around it. At some time during your years as a student, you'll have to face the dreaded "R" monster.

Nothing strikes more fear in the hearts of students everywhere. The thought of spending hours in the library digging up information...writing a long, detailed report... typing footnotes. For heaven's sake—if it's not enough to bring on actual terror, it certainly qualifies for mild panic!

"How will I get it all done?" you think. "Where do I start?" And, no doubt, "Why *me?*"

The fact that you picked up this book means you already have encountered the "R" monster, or expect to meet up with it all too soon. (I'm not naive enough to believe that you would actually *want* to write a research paper *just for the heck of it*—although that *would* be a valuable exercise.)

So let me reassure you right off: You will get it done. You will get a great grade on it. You will even learn a few things along the way. How? With the help of this book. I've been there. I'll show you my "tricks of the trade," every step of the way.

Step-by-step to success

Remember the old adage that "a journey of a thousand miles begins with a single step?" Well, so does the process of writing your research paper. The secret is to take things one step at a time. By breaking your assignment—no matter how huge or time-consuming a project—into a series of small steps, you'll turn a conceivably immense undertaking into a series of very manageable jobs.

First, in Chapter 1, you'll learn about the different elements that make up a research paper. I'll show you how to put together a work schedule *and* give you some tips on time-management.

In Chapter 2, I'll help you decide on a specific topic... and show you the kinds of topics to avoid like sour milk. I'll also show you how to develop a specific research angle or research argument—your *thesis*—and produce a preliminary outline for your paper.

Then, in Chapters 3, 4 and 5, we'll head for the library. You'll learn where to look for reference materials, a great system for keeping track of the reference materials you use, and a special note-taking system. You'll quickly be transformed into a more efficient, organized researcher—and get *more* done in *less* time.

In Chapters 6 and 7, you'll begin the actual writing of your paper. I'll show you some tricks that will help you organize it, some tips on overcoming writer's block, and a checklist to make sure you avoid plagiarizing. By the end of Chapter 7, you'll already have written a rough draft.

In Chapter 8, we'll discuss the various methods you can use to document your sources of information—*when* you must document a source, and *how* to do it.

Next, in Chapter 9, we'll edit your rough draft. You'll learn special strategies that will make your writing better, smoother, clearer.

You'll learn the ins and outs of putting together a bibliography—a list of the reference materials you used to write your paper—in Chapter 10. I'll give you the lowdown on all the rules you need to follow.

Finally, in Chapter 11, you'll learn some super proof-reading tricks so you catch *every* typographical error and spelling mistake in your paper. And voilà! You'll be on your way to class, finished masterpiece in hand!

You'll thank them later—really!

Yes, you're right. Doing a research paper means a lot of work. But the payoff is great, too. In addition to the obvious benefit—learning a lot about your research subject—you'll develop important skills every step of the way. You'll learn, for example:

1. How to track down information about *any* subject.

2. How to sort through that information and come to a conclusion about your subject.

3. How to prepare an organized, in-depth report.

4. How to communicate your ideas clearly and effectively.

Once you develop these skills, you own them.

You'll be able to apply them in *all* your high-school or college classes. They'll come in handy not only when you prepare other research papers, but also when you tackle smaller writing assignments, such as essays and oral reports.

When you graduate, these same skills will help you get ahead in the work world—the ability to analyze a subject and communicate through the written word are keys to success, no matter what career you choose.

Your teacher really didn't ask you to write a research paper just to make your life miserable. Of all the things you'll learn in school, the skills you acquire as we produce your research paper will be among the most valuable.

How to use this book

The steps I outline throughout this book are somewhat flexible. After you've "notched your pen" with one or two papers, you may want to adapt these steps a bit to fit your personal work style.

That's fine, just *don't skip any step altogether*. You may not understand the benefits of a particular step until you're further along in the process. So trust me. If you skip a step, you'll inevitably make your life more difficult in the long run.

Let's get started

Writing a research paper takes time, serious thought and effort. It is *not* easy. I can't change that any more than I can change your teacher's mind about assigning the paper in the first place.

But I *can* tell you that if you follow the steps outlined in this book, you'll find that the "R" monster is not such a terrifying creature after all. And I can guarantee that you will learn some things along the way that will profit you for the rest of your life.

It won't be painless, but at least the operation will be a success!

Chapter 1

A Look At The Job(s) Ahead

You may be only writing *one* paper, but there are actually *three* different jobs ahead of you:

First, you must be an ***objective reporter***—you'll dig up all the facts you can about your subject, gathering statistics, historical data, first-person accounts and more.

You will read reference books, newspaper stories, magazine articles, scholarly journals and other materials, watch a relevant video or film, even interview a real-live expert or two.

Your job is to find out the truth, to gather data with an unbiased eye.

You can't discard or ignore information just because it doesn't fit into the neat framework your personal opinions and expectations have constructed.

Second, you must be a *detective.*

Like a scientist evaluating the results of an experiment, you must review the evidence, decide what it does and doesn't mean, and draw the obvious (and, perhaps, not-so-obvious) conclusions.

Third, you must be an *author,* ready to share your new-found knowledge.

Having sifted through reams of information, you will write a cogent, well-thought-out, in-depth report, telling your readers what you have learned.

This is an exciting process—where else can you play three such different roles in a matter of weeks?—but one that demands some organization.

Create a work schedule

Doing all these tasks efficiently and effectively requires careful timing and planning. After all, this isn't the only assignment, or even the only paper, you have to get done in a short amount of time.

So get out your calendar and mark the date your paper is due. How many weeks till then? Four? Six? Ten? Plan to spend half of that time on research, the other half on writing.

Now, block out set periods of time during each week to work on your paper. Try to schedule large chunks of time —two, three hours or more at a shot—rather than many short periods. Otherwise, you'll spend most of your time "reviewing" where you left off and repeating steps unnecessarily.

As you make up your work schedule, set deadlines for completing the general steps of your paper-writing process. For example:

Week 1:	Decide on topic and "angle" of your paper.
Week 2:	Make list of reference materials.
Weeks 3/4:	Read reference materials; take notes.
Weeks 5/6:	Do detailed outline; write first draft.
Week 7:	Edit paper; prepare bibliography.
Week 8:	Proofread paper; type final copy.

Of course, I can't tell you exactly how much time to set aside for each step, because I don't know any of the specifics about your paper—how long it's supposed to be, how complex the topic, etc.—or how fast you work. I *can* tell you that you should plan on consulting and/or taking notes from at least 10 different books, articles or other reference materials. (Your teacher or subject may demand even *more;* I doubt you'll need fewer.) And you should plan on writing two or three drafts of your paper before you arrive at the final copy.

Refer to your work schedule often, and adjust your pace if you find yourself lagging behind.

Work smarter, not harder

Mastering "time management" does not require the brain of a rocket scientist—it just means *making the most of your time.* And that means planning ahead—for example, instead of making 15 short trips to the library, plan five or six extended research periods. You'll save travel time and footwork and get a lot more done in the same period of time.

Be prepared. Stock up on pencils, typewriter ribbons, computer disks and any other work supplies you need. Otherwise, you may find yourself running to the store at midnight in search of an elusive printer ribbon.

And *stay* organized. Keep all materials related to your paper in a separate notebook or file. No messy piles of work scattered here and there, just waiting to be lost or thrown away by mistake.

For a look at "everything you ever wanted to know" about time management, pick up a copy of *Manage Your Time*, another of the five books in my **HOW TO STUDY Program.**

And don't procrastinate!

Do not, I repeat, do *not* put off doing your research paper until the last minute—or even until the last week! If you do, you will make your task much more difficult. And probably wind up with a lousy paper, too.

Start working on your assignment now. *Right* now.

Chapter 2

Planning Your Attack

You're ready to take the first and conceivably most important step on the road to your A$^+$ research paper: deciding on a subject.

Once you've chosen a *general* area of study, you must target a *specific* topic or research question. Then, you need to come up with a general outline—a sketchy blueprint of your paper.

In this chapter, I'll help you complete all three tasks.

Choosing your topic

In some cases, your teacher will assign your topic. In others, your teacher will assign a general area of study, and you'll have the freedom to pick a specific topic.

With freedom sometimes comes danger—give this decision long and careful thought. Pick the wrong topic, and you can walk yourself right into disaster.

I'm not implying that you should pick the simplest topic you can find—simple topics often lead to simply awful papers. But there are definitely some pitfalls you must avoid.

Danger #1: Thinking too big

You need to write a 15-page paper for your American history class and decide your topic will be "America's Role in World War II."

Whoa! Think about it: Can you really cover a topic that broad in *15* pages? Not unless you simply rehash the high points, *à la* your third-grade history book. You could write volumes on the subject (people have) and still have plenty left to say!

Instead, you need to focus on a particular, limited aspect of your subject or attack it from a specific angle. Rather then "America's Role in World War II," how about "The Role of the Women Air Force Service Pilots in World War II?"

Remember, your job is to prepare an *in-depth* report about your subject. Be sure you can do that in the number of pages your teacher has requested.

Danger #2: Thinking too small

By the same token, you must not focus too narrowly. Choose a subject that's too limited, and you might run out of things to say on the second page of your paper. "The Design of the Women Air Force Service Pilots' Insignia" might make an interesting one- or two-page story, but it won't fill 10 or 15 pages...even with *really* wide margins.

Danger #3: Trodding the lonesome trail

Pick a topic that's too obscure, and you may find that little or no information has been written about it. In which case, you will have to conduct your own experiments... interview your own research subjects...and come up with your own, original data.

That is, of course, how scientists forge new pathways into the unknown. But I'm guessing that you have neither the time, desire, nor experience to take a similar start-from-scratch approach.

The point is: Make sure that there is enough research material available about your topic. And make sure that there are enough *different* sources of material—different authors, different books, etc.—so you can get a well-rounded view of your subject (and not be forced for lack of other material to find ways to make somebody else's points sound like your own).

Make a possibilities list

Taking all of the above into consideration, do a little brainstorming now about possible topics for your paper. Don't stop with the first idea—come up with several different possibilities.

In fact, put this book down and go make a list of three or four potential topics right now.

Do some preliminary research

Got your list? Then get thee to a library. You need to do a little advance research.

Skim through your library's card-catalog index, *Readers' Guide to Periodical Literature,* and other publication indexes. How many books and articles have been written about each topic on your "possibilities" list? Read a short background article or encyclopedia entry about each topic.

By the time you leave the library, you should have a general understanding of each of your potential subjects. You also should know whether you'll have trouble finding information about any topic on your list. If so, eliminate it.

Pick a winner

With any luck at all, you should be left with at least one topic that looks like a good research subject. If two or more topics passed your preliminary-research test, pick the one that interests you most.

You're going to spend a lot of time learning about your subject. There's no rule that says you can't enjoy it!

Develop a temporary thesis

Once you have chosen the topic for your paper, you must develop a *temporary thesis.*

What's a *thesis?* The word "thesis" is a relative of "hypothesis"—and means about the same thing: the central argument you will attempt to prove or disprove in your paper. It is the conclusion you draw about your subject, based upon your research.

A thesis is not the same thing as a *topic.* Your topic is what you study; your thesis is the conclusion you draw from that study.

A *thesis statement* is a one-sentence summary of your thesis, summing up the main point of your paper.

Suppose you decided that the topic of your paper will be "The Role of the Women Air Force Service Pilots in World War II." At the end of your research, you have concluded that the pilots played a very valuable role in the war effort. Your thesis statement, then, might be:

The Women Air Force Service Pilots played an important role in World War II.

In your paper, you would try to prove this thesis, explaining why the contributions of the pilots were so important.

Temporary means just that

Note that word *temporary*. No matter how good it looks to you now, your temporary thesis may *not* wind up being your final thesis. Because you haven't completed all your research yet, you can only come up with a "best-guess" thesis at this point.

You may find out during your research that your temporary thesis is all wet. If that's the case, you will revise it, perhaps even settling on a thesis that's the exact opposite of your first! In fact, you may revise your thesis *several* times during the course of your research.

If a temporary thesis doesn't spring easily to mind—and it probably won't—sit back, and do some more brainstorming. Ask yourself questions like:

- "What's special or unusual about _____ ?" (Fill in the blank with your topic.)
- "How is _____ related to events in the past?"
- "What impact has _____ made on society?"
- "What would I like the world to know about _____ ?"
- "What questions do I have about _____ ?"

The answers to these and similar questions should lead you to several good thesis ideas. If you find yourself needing more information about your topic to answer these questions, go back to the library and do a bit more reading.

Ask your instructor

Some teachers require you to submit your thesis statement for their approval prior to beginning your paper. Even if this is *not* required, getting your instructor's opinion is always a good idea. He or she will help you determine whether your thesis argument is on target, and, if not, perhaps how to fix it.

Create a temporary outline

Once you have developed your temporary thesis, think about how you might approach the subject in your paper. Jot down the various issues you plan to investigate. Then, come up with a brief, temporary outline of your paper, showing the order in which you might discuss those issues.

Let's suppose your temporary thesis was: "Even though they served as civilians, the Women Air Force Service Pilots of WWII deserved to be given official status as veterans."

Based on what you learned in your preliminary research, your temporary outline might look like this:

A. Why civilian women pilots entered the war

B. The type and number of women who participated

C. Their qualifications and training

D. Their missions and contributions

E. The military vs. civilian status question

F. The disbanding of the group

G. The fight to be recognized as veterans

Don't worry too much about this outline—it will be brief, at best. It's simply a starting point for your research, a plan of attack.

But don't skip this step, either. As you'll find out in later chapters, it will be a big help in organizing your research findings.

Chapter 3

Research, Phase 1: The Hunt

You've accomplished a lot so far: You've determined your topic of study. You've developed a temporary thesis. And you've created a temporary outline for your paper. Congratulations!

Now it's time to begin your research in earnest.

We're going to tackle this initial information hunt in two phases. First, you'll come up with a list of all the books, magazines and other research materials you want to consult.

Then, you'll sit down and do the actual reading and note-taking.

In Chapter 4, I'll show you a time-saving way to compile and organize your reading list. And in Chapter 5, I'll teach you an efficient way to take notes.

But first, you need to learn where and how to locate the many different kinds of research materials you can consult.

Into the library

The obvious place to begin your hunt for research materials is the library. Today's libraries offer an amazing variety of resources—learn how to tap into their gold mine of information and you'll be much richer.

I'm going to assume that you already have some knowledge of how to use the library. If you have gotten this far in life *without* being introduced to library basics, just ask your librarian for help. (As a matter of fact, even if you consider yourself something of a library expert, always ask your librarian for help! Make the "information" desk a regular hangout. Tell the librarians what you're working on—they'll invariably know the best sources of information and where to find them.)

At most libraries, many of those old, familiar library tools—like the trusty card catalog—have been replaced by computerized systems. These can be a little intimidating for first-time users, but they are great time-savers. Again, don't be shy about asking for help. Your librarian will be happy to show you how to make the computers work their magic.

Beyond the encyclopedia

When you were younger, you probably relied solely on the encyclopedias in your school library when you had to write a report. Sorry, but those simpler, easier days are gone for good.

Yes, you may want to read encyclopedias to get a general overview of your topic. But you need to turn to other sources for more detailed information. You need to read books written by experts in the field you're researching, and magazine and newspaper articles about every aspect of your subject.

Why stop there? Pamphlets...brochures...government documents...specialized anthologies...films and videos... these are just some of the other possible sources of information for your paper.

Where to look for materials

How do you find out whether anyone has written a magazine or newspaper article about your topic? How do you know if there are any government documents or pamphlets that might be of help? How do you locate those written-by-the-experts reference books?

You look in your library's publication indexes, which list all of the articles, books and other materials that have been published and/or are available in your library. Most are arranged alphabetically by subject.

Be sure to look under more than one subject heading when you search for reference materials. For example, if we were looking for resources for our World War II paper, we might look under "Women in Aviation," "Veterans— Women," and "World War II."

Some of the major publication indexes are listed below. There are others—ask your librarian for suggestions.

> 1. *The Card Catalog:* This is a list of all the books in your library. (Although many libraries now store it on computer, it's still often called a card catalog because it used to be kept on index cards.) Books are indexed in three different ways: by subject, by author and by title.

2. *Newspaper Indexes:* Several large-city newspapers provide an indexed list of all articles they have published.

3. *Periodical Indexes:* To find out if any magazine articles have been published on your subject, go to a periodical index. *The Readers' Guide to Periodical Literature,* which indexes articles published in the most popular American magazines, may be one with which you're familiar.

4. *Vertical File:* Here's where you'll find pamphlets and brochures.

5. *U.S. Documents Monthly Catalog:* Useful for locating government publications.

Other ideas

When you're making up your list of possible reference materials (which you'll learn how to do in the next chapter), you also may want to check the following:

1. *Special Anthologies, Almanacs and Encyclopedias:* Providing more in-depth information than general encyclopedias, these are entire series devoted exclusively to specific topics.

2. *Association Directories:* An association or organization related to your topic can be one of your most valuable sources of information. Often, such organizations have a historian who can provide you with extensive literature—or, better yet, the names of experts whom you might interview! You can find their names and addresses here.

One more time...

Remember, all these resources are just a starting point for your hunt for reference materials. There are many other excellent resources you will need to check. Many libraries print a list of such resources and a map of where they can be found.

What if yours doesn't? That's right—ask your librarian for help.

You *were* paying attention, weren't you?

On to chapter 4.

The Working Bibliography

Working bibliography? "Ugh," you think, "sounds complicated."

Relax. Remember what I told you in Chapter 3—the first step of your research is to put together a list of books, magazines, pamphlets, etc., you want to read. "Working bibliography" is simply a fancy name for that list.

There are two steps involved. First, you'll create bibliography cards for each source of information you want to review. Then, you'll transfer all the information from your bibliography cards to a single list—your working bibliography.

This two-step method has been around since man wrote the first research paper, and with good reason: It works! It helps you conduct your research in an organized, efficient manner *and* makes preparing your final bibliography easier.

In other words, this is one of those great time-saving tools that I promised to show you!

This is not a complicated job, but it is an important one. So follow my instructions to the letter.

Essential ingredients: 3-by-5 index cards

To create your working bibliography, you'll need a supply of 3-by-5 index cards. You can buy these for next to nothing at most dime stores, bookstores and office stores. (You'll also use index cards when you take notes for your paper, so buy a big batch now. A few hundred cards ought to suffice.)

While you're stocking up on index cards, pick up one of those little envelope files designed to hold the cards. Put your name, address and phone number on the file. If you lose it, some kind stranger may return it.

Step 1: Create your bibliography cards

You'll complete the first step of the bibliography two-step at the library. Take your index cards, a couple of pens or pencils—and this book, of course.

Start a systematic search for any materials that might have information related to your paper. Look through the indexes we covered in Chapter 3 and any other indexes your librarian recommends.

When you find a book, article or other resource that looks promising, take out a blank note card. On the front of the card, write down the following information:

In the upper right-hand corner of the card: The library call number (Dewey decimal number or Library of Congress number), if there is one. Add any other detail that will help you locate the material on the library shelves (e.g. "Science Reading Room," "Reference Room," "Micro-fiche Periodicals Room").

On the main part of the card: The author's name, if given—last name first, first name, middle name or ini-tial. Then the title of the article, if applicable, in quotation marks. Then the name of the book, magazine, newspaper or other publication—underlined.

Add any details you will need if you have to find the book or article again, e.g.:

- Date of publication
- Edition—e.g., "third (1990) edition" for a book; "morning edition" for a newspaper.
- Volume number
- Page numbers on which the article or in-formation appears

In the upper left-hand corner of the card: Number it. The first card you write will be #1, the second, #2, and so on. If you happen to mess up and skip a number some-where along the line, don't worry. It's only important that you assign a different number to each card.

At the bottom of the card: If you're going to be working in more than one library, write the name of the library. Also write down the name of the index in which you found the resource, in case you need to refer to it again.

Do this for *each* potential source of information you find. *And put only one resource on each card.*

Some experts in the research-paper business have different ideas about what goes where on bibliography cards. It's not really important—if you prefer to put the elements of your card in some different order, it's okay.

Just be sure that you're consistent, so you'll know what's what later on. And leave some room on the card— you'll be adding more information when you actually get the reference material in your hands.

Sample Bibliography Card For A Book

```
(1)                                    315.6
                            Main Reading Room

            Jones, Karen A.
    The Life and Times of Bob Smith.
            (see esp. pp. 43-48)


                Card Catalog
            Main Street Library
```

Sample Bibliography Card
For A Magazine Article

```
(2)                          Periodical Room

                Perkins, Stan
     "The Life and Times of Bob Smith"
             Smith Magazine
        (April 24, 1989; pp. 22-26)


                Readers' Guide
             University Library
```

Sample Bibliography Card
For A Newspaper Article

```
(3)                           Microfiche Room

            Black, Bill
   "Bob Smith: The New Widget Spinner"
            New York Times
   (June 16, 1976, late edition, p. A12)


         New York Times Index
         Main Street Library
```

Evaluating resources

You may find so many potential resources that you know you won't have time to read them all. If so, concentrate on those that have been published most recently or written by the most respected sources.

However, don't limit yourself *too* much—you should gather information from a wide range of sources. Otherwise, you may wind up learning only one side of the story.

Primary vs. secondary resources

There are two basic types of resources: ***primary*** and ***secondary***.

Primary resources are written by people who *actually witnessed or participated in an event*. When you read a scientist's report about an experiment he has conducted, you are consulting a primary resource.

Secondary resources are written by people *who were not actually present at an event,* but have studied the subject. When you read a book about the 1950s written by someone who was born in 1960, you are learning from a secondary resource.

Obviously, primary resources are likely to be more reliable sources of information. But depending upon your subject, there may not *be* any primary resources available to you.

Step 2: Prepare your working bibliography

When you get home, copy the information from each of your bibliography cards onto a single list. As you do this, follow the bibliography style rules outlined in Chapter 10. (These rules cover bibliographic minutiae—where to put periods, how many spaces to indent lines, etc.) When you've finished your list—your working bibliography— make a photocopy or two. Keep one copy with your research file, another in a safe place in your room or desk.

Although you'll work from your bibliography cards as you conduct your research, your working bibliography is important for two reasons:

1. You'll have a separate record of all the potential resources you found. If you lose any of your bibliography cards, you can recreate it easily.

2. You'll be able to use your working bibliography as the basis for your final one.

The final bibliography, a required part of your paper, lists resources from which you gathered information. Your *working* bibliography contains all the resources from which you *might* gather information.

Okay, so why the card game?

Why bother to create all those separate bibliography cards if you're just going to transfer the information to another piece of paper? It's a matter of convenience and organization. With index cards, you can organize your list of resources in different ways, just by shuffling the deck.

For example, you might want to start by organizing your cards by resource: magazine articles, encyclopedias, books, newspapers, etc. Then, when you're in the magazine room of the library, you will have a quick and easy way to make sure you read all your magazine articles at the same time. Ditto for your trip to the newspaper reading room, the reference shelf, and so on.

But at some point, you might want to have your list of resources organized in alphabetical order. Or separated into piles of resources you've checked, and those you haven't. No problem: Just shuffle your cards again.

Even with the help of a computer, it would be time-consuming to do all of this on paper. The note-card system is neater and more efficient. And that's the key to getting your work done as quickly and painlessly as possible!

Chapter 5

Research, Phase 2: Digging In

Did you ever dream of sleuthing about like Agatha Christie? Or "breaking" a front-page story like Woodward & Bernstein? If you ever thought being a detective or investigative reporter could be fun, then get ready to have some! It's time to follow up all of those research leads you found, track down the evidence, and uncover the truth, the whole truth, and nothing but the truth.

In other words, it's time to start taking notes.

When you write your paper, you'll work from your notes, not the original reference materials. Why? Because it's easier to turn a few cards than flip through hundreds of pages in search of the information you need. Because it's easier than lugging home stacks of heavy books from the library. And because you don't have a choice—many of the materials you may need to consult can't be taken *out* of the library!

In this chapter, I'm going to show you my own special system for taking notes. Master it—it will be a huge help when you sit down to organize and write your paper.

Send for information/schedule interviews

Before you do anything else, send away for anything you want to review that isn't available in your library. If you want to get a brochure from a particular association, for example, order it now. It may take a few weeks for such materials to arrive.

If you're going to interview any experts, schedule interview dates with them. Make up a list of good questions, and buy or borrow a quality tape recorder so you can accurately record your interviewee's comments.

Then hit the books

Set aside solid blocks of time for your library work. And remember: It's better to schedule a handful of extended trips to the library than 15 or 20 brief visits.

When you go to the library, take your bibliography cards, a good supply of blank index cards, your preliminary outline and several pens or pencils.

Your bibliography cards are the map for your information treasure hunt. When you arrive at the library, pull out the first five or six cards, locate the materials listed on them, pick a secluded desk or table, and get to work.

How to take notes

What sort of information should you put in your notes? Anything related to your subject and especially to your thesis: general background information—names, dates, historical data, etc.; research statistics; quotes by experts; and definitions of technical terms.

You may be used to keeping your notes in a three-ring binder or notepad. I'm going to show you an I think is better—you'll record all of your notes on your blank index cards.

As was the case with your bibliography cards, you must follow some specific guidelines to make this method work. You'll want to refer to the guidelines in this chapter often during your first few note-taking sessions. After that, the system will become second nature to you.

Step #1: Complete the bibliography card

Let's say that you have found a reference book that contains some information about your subject. Before you begin taking notes, get out the bibliography card for that book.

First, check that all of the information on your card is correct. Is the title exactly as printed on the book? Is the author's name spelled correctly?

Next, add any other information you will need to include in your final bibliography. The type of information you need to put on your bibliography card depends on two factors: 1) The type of reference material and 2) the bibliography format you are required to use.

Various authorities have set forth a bewildering array of bibliography rules. While none of them are inherently "right" or "wrong," be sure to ask your instructor which rules he or she wants you to follow.

In this book, we'll cover the bibliography gospel according to the Modern Language Association of America (MLA), one of the most widely accepted authorities on such matters.

Unfortunately, even when using only one set of rules, there are different instructions for different types of materials. You handle a bibliography listing for a video differently than you do for a book, for instance. If I were to show you how to handle all the different types of materials you might encounter, this book would easily be three times as large.

And it would be a waste of time and paper, because there are several books already on the market that *do* show every type of listing under the sun. (The MLA, for example, puts out its own very thorough reference manual.) You may want to consult one of these books if you're working with out-of-the-ordinary types of reference materials. Just make sure that the book that you consult follows the bibliography format your teacher requires.

Because most students rely heavily on books, magazine articles and newspaper articles for research, I'll give you the rules for those materials here.

Bibliography listings typically include three categories of information: the author's name, the title of the work, and the publishing information. However, there are lots of little pieces of data that fall within those three categories. Include on your card the following information, in the following order:

For a book:

1. *Name(s) of the author(s)*
2. *Title of the part of the book* used (if the entire book does not deal with your subject), in quotes
3. *Title of the book,* underlined
4. Name of the *editor, translator or compiler*

5. *Edition used,* if more than one edition has been published (If you don't see any information about an edition, assume it's the first.)

6. Number of *volume(s) used,* if more than one

7. Name of the *series,* if the book is part of one

8. *Place of publication, name of the publisher, date of publication*

9. If pertinent information appears in only a small portion of the book, the *page numbers* on which it appears

10. *Supplementary information*—any other details needed to identify the exact book you used (e.g., "Spanish language translation")

You generally will find all this information on the book's cover, title page and/or copyright page.

For an article in a periodical (magazines, newspapers, etc.:

1. *Name(s) of the author(s)*

2. *Title of the article,* in quotation marks

3. *Name of the periodical,* underlined. (If you are working with a newspaper that is not widely known or nationally published, put the name of the city or town in which it is published. For example: The Herald [Lawrence, NJ].)

4. *Series number or name,* if one is given;

5. *Volume number* Include this only if you are working with a scholarly journal. If you're not sure whether a periodical is considered a "scholarly journal," ask your librarian or go ahead and include the volume number just in case.

6. *Date of publication* Include the edition of a newspaper, if there is more than one— i.e., morning or evening edition, early or late edition, etc.

7. The *page numbers* on which the article appears. Include the section letter or number for a newspaper: A8, B12, etc.

For a magazine, look for this information on the front cover and within the article itself. For a newspaper, look at the front page and within the article.

Of course, not every bibliography card will include all of these details. Some books may not have an editor, for example. You don't need to write "no editor" on the card; simply move on to the next applicable piece of information.

Step #2: Write your note cards

Once your first bibliography card is finished, set it aside. Get out some blank index cards, and start taking notes from your reference source. Follow these guidelines:

• *Write one thought, idea, quote or fact on each card.* If you encounter a very long quote or string of data, you can write on both the front and back of a card, if necessary. *But never carry over a note to a second card.*

What if you simply *can't* fit the piece of information on one card? You're dealing with too much information at once. Break it down into two or more smaller pieces, then put each on a separate card.

- ***Write in your own words.*** Summarize key points about a paragraph or section. Or, restate the material in your own words. Avoid copying things word for word.

- ***Put quotation marks around any material copied verbatim.*** It's okay to include in your paper a sentence or paragraph written by someone else to emphasize a particular point (providing you do so on a limited basis). But you must copy such statements *exactly as written* in the original—every word, every comma, every period. You also must *always* put such direct quotes within quotation marks.

Add organizational details

As you finish each note card, do the following:

- ***In the upper left-hand corner of the card:*** Write down the resource number of the corresponding bibliography card (in its left-hand corner). This will remind you where you got the information.

- ***Below the resource number:*** Write the page number(s) on which the information appeared.

- Get out your preliminary outline. Under which outline topic heading does the information on your note card seem to fit? Under your "A" heading? Under "C?" *Jot the appropriate topic letter in the upper right-hand corner of your note card.*

If you're not sure where the information fits into your outline, put an asterisk (*) instead of a topic letter. Later, when you do a more detailed outline, you can try to fit these "miscellaneous" note cards into specific areas.

- *Next to the topic letter:* Jot down a one- or two-word "headline" that describes the information on the card. For example, if your note card contains a statistic on how many women pilots were killed in WWII, your headline might be: "Casualties—Statistics."

- *When you have finished taking notes from a particular resource,* put a check mark on the bibliography card. This will let you know that you're done with that resource.

Be sure that you transfer information accurately to your note cards.

Double-check names, dates and other statistics.

As with your bibliography cards, it's not vital that you put each of these elements in the *exact* places I've outlined above. You just need to be consistent.

Always put the page number in the same place, in the same manner. Ditto with the resource number, the topic heading and the headline.

On the next page, I've included a sample of a completed note card to which you can refer.

Sample Completed Note Card

```
(2)                                  C
p. 22              Education—Degrees

Smith awarded honorary degrees in
law from both Harvard & Princeton
```

Add your personal notes

Throughout your note-taking process, you may want to make some "personal" note cards—your own thoughts, ideas or impressions about your subject or your thesis.

Perhaps you've thought of a great introduction for your paper. Put it on a card. Or maybe you've thought of a personal experience that relates to your topic. Put it on a card.

Write each thought on a separate note card, just as you have with information you've taken from other resources. And assign your note card a topic heading and mini-headline, too. In the space where you would normally put the number of the resource, put your own initials. This will remind you that *you* were the source of the information or thought.

Keep an eye out for new resources

When you look up information in one reference book, you'll often find leads to additional resources. Check to see if these resources are on your working bibliography. If not, and you think they are worth consulting, add them. Make up a bibliography card for each new source, too.

Throw away unprofitable leads

If a particular resource doesn't yield any useful information, take the bibliography card for that resource out of your stack. Stick it away in your card file, just in case you want it later.

Or, if you're certain that you won't want to refer back to the resource, throw the bibliography card away altogether. Then scratch the listing from your working bibliography. You don't need to renumber your remaining cards—it doesn't matter if a number is missing.

Why are you doing all this?

Of all the tips you'll learn in this book, this note-taking system is undoubtedly one of the most valuable. In fact, it's one that many *professional* writers swear by.

When you go to write your final bibliography, you'll have all the information you need on your bibliography cards. No trips back to the library to look up bibliography details! You just put your cards in the order that they will appear in your bibliography, and copy the information.

But the biggest benefit of the system is that it helps you organize your findings and makes your writing job easier.

You'll find out *how* easy in the next chapter.

Chapter 6

Organizing Your Research

Your research is done.

Which means—if you managed your time as I suggested earlier—that fully *one half* of your *paper* is done, even though you've yet to write one word of the first draft!

You've finished going through all of those reference materials listed in your working bibliography.

You've completed your bibliography cards.

You've uncovered a lot of information about your subject.

And you've taken extensive notes.

It's time to organize your data.

You need to decide if your temporary thesis is still on target, determine how you will organize your paper, and create a detailed outline.

Review your thesis statement

Take a close look at your temporary thesis statement.

Does it still make sense, given all the information your research has revealed?

If it doesn't, revise it.

Your research should have led you to *some* conclusion about your subject. This, in turn, should lead you to the final thesis of your paper.

Sort your note cards

Once you have your final thesis, begin thinking about how you will organize your paper. This is where the note-card system you learned in Chapter 5 really pays off. Get out all of your note cards, then:

- Group together all of the cards that share the same outline topic letter (in the upper right-hand corner of each card).

- Put those different groups in order, according to your temporary outline—topic "A" cards on top, followed by topic "B" cards, then topic "C" cards, etc.

- Within each topic group, sort the cards further. Put together all of the cards that share the same "headline"—the two-word title in the upper-right hand corner.

- Go through your miscellaneous topic cards—those marked with an asterisk. Can you fit any of them into your existing topic groups? If so, replace the asterisk with the topic letter. If not, put the card at the very back of your stack.

Decide on the order of your paper

Your note cards now should be organized according to your preliminary outline. Take a few minutes to read through your note cards, beginning at the front of the stack and moving through to the back. *What you are reading is a sketchy draft of your paper*—the information you collected in the order you (temporarily) plan to present it.

Now, consider: Does that order still make sense? Or would another arrangement work better? For example, perhaps you had planned to use chronological order—to tell readers what happened, in the order that it happened. After reviewing your note cards, you may decide that it would be better to take a cause/effect approach—to discuss, one by one, a series of different events and explain the impact of each.

Here are some of the different organizational approaches you might consider for your paper:

1. *Chronological*—discusses events in the order in which they happened (by time or date of occurrence)

2. *Spatial*—presents information in geographical or physical order (from north to south, largest to smallest, etc.)

3. *Cause/effect*—one by one, discusses the effects of a series of individual events or actions

4. *Problem/solution*—presents a series of problems and possible solutions

5. *Compare/contrast*—discusses the similarities and differences between people, things or events

6. *Order of importance*—discusses the most
   important aspects of an issue first and
   continues through to the least important

Your subject matter and your thesis may well determine which of these organizational approaches will work
best. If you have a choice of more than one, use the one
with which you're most comfortable or that you feel will be
easiest for you to write. (Nobody says you *have* to choose
the hardest way!) And keep in mind that you can use a
blend of two approaches—for example, you might mention
events in chronological order and then discuss the cause/
effect of each.

Re-sort your cards

If necessary, revise your general outline according to
the organizational decision you just made. However, *don't*
change the letters that you have assigned to the topics in
your outline. (If you decide to put topic "B" first in your
new outline, keep using the letter "B" in front of it.) Otherwise, the topic letters on your note cards won't match
those on your outline.

If you revised your outline, re-order your note cards so
that they fall in the same order as your new outline.

Now, go through each group of cards that share the
same topic letter. Rearrange them so that they, too, follow
the organizational pattern you chose.

For an example of how this works, let's stay with our
paper on women pilots in World War II. If you remember,
the "A" topic on our general outline was: "Why civilian
women pilots entered the war."

When we took notes, we assigned the following headlines to various "A" note cards: "Women pilot proposal,"
"Shortage of male pilots," and "Test program approved."

If we decided to use chronological order for our paper, we would shuffle our "A" note cards accordingly—cards marked "Shortage of male pilots" would go first, because the shortage was the first thing that happened. All cards marked "Women pilot proposal" come next, followed by cards marked "Test program begun."

Add any miscellaneous cards

After you sort all the cards that have been assigned a specific topic heading, review cards that are still marked with an asterisk. Try to fit them in your stack of cards.

Don't force a note card in. If there doesn't seem to be any logical place for the information on the card, it may be that the data just isn't relevant to your thesis. Set the card aside in a "leftover" pile. You can try again later.

Your detailed outline is done!

Flip through your note cards from front to back. See that? You've created a detailed outline without even knowing it. The topic letters on your note cards match the main topics of your outline. And those headlines on your note cards? They're the subtopics for your outline.

For example, the first part of our detailed outline for our "women pilots" paper would be:

A. Why civilian women pilots entered the
   war effort
   1. Shortage of male pilots
   2. Women pilot proposal
   3. Test program begun

We simply transferred our note-card headlines to paper—they appear on our outline in the same order as they appear in our stack of cards.

Some instructors like to approve your outline before letting you proceed with your paper. If yours does, find out the specific outline format you are to follow. You may need to use a different numbering/lettering format from the one shown above—Roman numerals instead of capital letters for topic headings, for example.

Otherwise, you can get as detailed as you like with your outline. In most cases, a two-level outline—with topic headings plus subheadings—will do. Remember that you must have at least two entries at every outline level.

Here's an example of a detailed outline for our "women pilots" paper, which presumes that we decided to organize our paper on chronological order:

Sample Detailed Outline

The Women's Air Force Service in World War II

A. Why civilian women pilots entered the war effort

    1. Shortage of male pilots

    2. Women pilot proposal

    3. Test program begun

B. The type and number of women who participated

    1. Statistics on number of initial participants

    2. Background information about leaders of the program

    3. Participants' socio-economic background

C. Their qualifications and training
   1. Experience needed to be accepted into the program
   2. Training program
      a. ground school
      b. flight school
      c. exams
D. Their missions and contributions
   1. Ferrying planes
   2. Towing targets
   3. Testing repaired planes
   4. Success vs. male pilots
E. The military vs. civilian status question
   1. Reason for initial civilian status
   2. Plan to militarize
   3. Why plan was needed
   4. Why plan was not carried out
F. The disbanding of the group
   1. Additional pilots no longer needed
   2. Male pilots wanted jobs taken over by women
   3. Support for/against disbanding
G. The fight to be recognized as veterans
   1. Importance of the fight
      a. veterans' benefits for the women
      b. recognition of the group's contributions
   2. Instrumental women in the fight
   3. Debate and vote in Congress
   4. Outcome and effect of vote

Now I get it!

If you haven't figured it out before, you should understand now why this note-card system is so valuable. If you had written all of your notes on several dozen sheets of paper, it would be quite a task to sort out information and to put it in some logical order, let alone re-order it at will.

And this isn't the only stage at which having your notes on individual cards comes in handy. As you'll see in Chapter 7, the note-card system also is helpful when you tackle the next phase of your paper: writing your rough draft.

Chapter 7

Writing Your Rough Draft

For some reason, this step is the hardest for most people. It's psychological, I guess—a fear that when your thoughts actually appear in black and white, there for all the world to read, you'll be judged a complete fool.

Well, you can't do a research paper without writing. And since the job has to be done, you might as well face it right now.

Using this book, you'll find this step a lot easier than your friends might. Assuming, of course, that you've done everything as instructed so far—taken good notes, organized your note cards, prepared a detailed outline, etc.

You may not have realized it, but you've already *done* a lot of the hard work that goes into the writing stage. You have thought about how your paper will flow. You have organized your notes. And you have prepared a detailed outline. All that's left is to transfer your information and ideas from note cards to paper.

Still, as a writer, I know that this can be a scary prospect, no matter how well you've done up to now . So, in this chapter, I'll show you some tips and tricks that will make writing your rough draft a bit easier.

Because the things you will learn in this chapter and Chapter 8 work together, read both chapters before you begin to write. Then come back and actually work through the steps outlined here.

Set the stage for good writing

Unfortunately for the party-lovers of this world, writing is a solitary activity. Good writing takes concentration and thought. And concentration and thought require quiet —and lots of it!

Find a quiet place to work, and do what you can to make sure you won't be interrupted. Nothing's more maddening than having the perfect phrase on the tip of your brain, only to have a friend pop in and wipe it out of your mind forever.

You also need to have plenty of desk space, so you can spread out your note cards. Your work area should be well lit. And you should have a dictionary and thesaurus close at hand. (And if you need even more help than this brief synopsis, get a copy of another book in my **HOW TO STUDY** *Program—Manage Your Time*—where all this is discussed in far more detail.)

If possible, work on a computer, so that you can add, delete and rearrange your words easily. Don't worry if your computer software doesn't have all the latest bells and whistles—a simple word-processing program is all you really need.

Don't psych yourself out

If you go into this thinking you're going to turn out a teacher-ready paper on your first try, you're doomed. That kind of performance pressure leads only to anxiety and frustration.

At this point, your goal is to produce a rough draft—with the emphasis on *rough*. Your first draft isn't *supposed* to be perfect. It's *supposed* to need revision.

Relax your expectations, and you'll find that ideas flow much more freely. You'll be surprised at the intelligent, creative thoughts that come out of that brain of yours when you're not so worried about making a mistake.

Thinking now, grammar later

The essence of good writing has little to do with grammar, spelling, punctuation and the like. The essence of good writing is good thinking.

Sure, the mechanics of writing are important. And you do need to make sure that you have everything spelled just right, that your participles aren't dangling, your periods and commas are placed just so.

But your thoughts, ideas and logic are the foundation of your paper. And you need to build a foundation before you worry about hanging the front door. So, for now, just concentrate on getting your thoughts on paper. Don't worry about using exactly the "right" word. Don't worry about getting commas in all the right places. We'll take care of all that polishing later.

Do a note card draft

Your note cards helped you come up with a detailed outline. Now, they're going to serve you again—helping you plot out the paragraphs and sentences of your paper.

We're going to do some more sorting and rearranging of cards. The end result will be what I call a "note card draft." Here's what you do:

1. Your note cards should be arranged in the same order as your detailed outline. Take out all of the note cards labeled with the letter of the first topic on your outline.

2. Out of that stack, take out all the cards marked with the same "headline" as the first subheading in your outline.

3. Look at the information on those cards, and think about how the various statistics, quotes and facts might fit together in a paragraph.

4. Rearrange those cards so they fall in the order you have determined is best for the paragraph.

5. Do this for each group of cards, until you reach the end of the deck.

To illustrate this process, let's use the example of our paper on women pilots.

Suppose we have 25 note cards with information related to the first topic heading in our outline—"Why civilian women pilots entered the war." And suppose that four of those 25 cards have information related to the first subtopic— "Shortage of male pilots."

Here's the information on each card:

Card #1: Quote from a general about the ser-
iousness of the pilot shortage

Card #2: Statistics about how many pilots were needed and the number available for active duty

Card #3: Brief explanation of why there was
a shortage

Card #4: Description of the type of jobs that
weren't getting done because of the
pilot shortage

How could we string these four pieces of information together into a paragraph or series of paragraphs? Here's one solution:

1. Start out with the statistic (card 2)

2. Explain reasons for the shortage (card 3)

3. Discuss the kind of jobs that needed to be filled (card 4)

4. Wrap up with the general's quote, which serves to summarize and emphasize the key point of the section (card 1)

This decided, we simply shuffle the note cards so that they fall in that order. Then we move on through the rest of our note cards, continuing to create new paragraphs, until our entire paper is mapped out.

Building good paragraphs

I don't want to get into a lengthy discussion of English composition here, but since we're dealing with how to build the paragraphs in your paper, it makes sense to stop for a brief discussion of what's involved in good paragraph construction.

Each paragraph in your paper is like a mini-essay. It should have a topic sentence—a statement of the key point or fact you will discuss in the paragraph—and contain the evidence to support it. You shouldn't expect your reader to believe that your topic sentence is true just because you say so—you must back up your point with hard data. This evidence can come in different forms, such as:

- Quotes from experts
- Research statistics
- Examples from research or from your own experience
- Detailed descriptions or other background information

Paragraphs are like bricks of information—stack them up, one by one, until you have built a wall of evidence. Construct each paragraph carefully, and your readers will have no choice but to agree with your final conclusion.

If paragraphs are the bricks in your wall of evidence, transitions—a sentence or phrase that moves the reader from one thought to another—are the mortar that holds them together. Smooth transitions help readers move effortlessly from the summary of one paragraph to the introduction of another. (The first sentence in the paragraph you have just read is an example of a transition.)

Now put it all on paper

It's time to take the plunge and turn your note card draft into a written rough draft. Using your cards as your guide, sit down and write.

Double- or triple-space your draft—that will make it easier to edit later. After you are finished with each note card, put a check mark at the bottom.

If you decide that you won't include information from a particular card, don't throw the card away—yet. Keep it in a separate stack. You may decide to fit in that piece of information in another part of your paper. Or change your mind after you read your rough draft and decide to include the information where you originally planned.

If you get stuck...

Got writer's block already? Here are a few tricks to get you unstuck:

- *Pretend you're writing to a good friend*—just tell him or her everything you've learned about your subject and why you believe your thesis is correct.

- *Use everyday language.* Too many people get so hung up on using fancy words and phrases that they forget that their goal is to *communicate.* Simpler is better.

- *Just do it.* What is it about a blank computer screen or piece of paper that scares would-be writers so badly? It happens to almost everyone, and there's only one cure I know: Just type something ...*any*-thing. Once you have written that first paragraph—even if it's a really *bad* first paragraph—your brain will start to generate spontaneous ideas.

- *Don't edit yourself!* As you write your rough draft, don't keep beating yourself up with negative thoughts such as "This sounds really stupid" or "I'm a terrible writer. Why can't I express that better?" Remember: Your goal is a *rough* draft—it's supposed to stink a bit.

- *Keep moving.* If you get hung up in a particular section, don't sit there stewing over it for hours—or even for many min-utes. Just write a quick note about what you plan to cover in that section, then go on to the next section.

For example: "Talk about how women pilots were ridiculed by men in the air forces at first. Mention instances quoted from resource #12. Add statistics that proved women could do the job."

- *If you can't get even that much out,* skip the section altogether and come back to it later. The point is, *do whatever you have to do to keep moving forward.* Force yourself to make it all the way through your paper, with as few stops as possible.

The trouble with plagiarism

It's so tempting. You're having trouble with a sentence or section. The information you need was explained beautifully in that article you found in an old magazine. Why not just copy the section from the article?

Because that would be plagiarism, that's why. And plagiarism—passing off another person's words or ideas as your own—is the biggest no-no of research-paper writing. It's a sure way to bring your grade down, down, down. It may even get you a failing mark.

"But who'll ever know that I didn't write it myself?" you wonder. Sorry, but the odds are about 999 to 1 that you *will* be found out.

First, your teacher probably has been reading research papers—some of them undoubtedly on the same subject as yours—for a good many years. Those same "perfect passages" tend to pop up again and again. Do you really think your teacher will believe it's a coincidence that you wrote the exact same paragraph as that student in *last* year's class? Who flunked, by the way.

Second, your teacher is familiar with your work and your writing style. That "borrowed" paragraph, written in someone else's style, is going to be noticeably different from your own deathless prose.

Then, of course, there is the moral issue involved—but I won't get into that. You learned that stealing was wrong in kindergarten. The principle applies to written words and ideas, too.

And how to avoid it

To avoid plagiarism, you must give proper credit to the original author of material you use. You must also give credit for any facts, figures or research data that you use. You do this through a *source note*—footnote, endnote or parenthetical note.

Sometimes, you might want to include a sentence or entire paragraph exactly as it was written by another author. If you do this, you must enclose the material in quotation marks and copy the material word for word, comma for comma. And you must offset the paragraph from the rest of the paper by indenting it from both margins, like this:

> "The author's paragraph is set off from the rest of the section by indenting it from both margins. It also is enclosed in quotation marks."

You should use this device sparingly, and only if the segment is so eloquently written or so meaningful that it makes a special impact on the reader.

You should *not* do this to fill up your paper "the easy way"—if your teacher is anything like most of mine were, he or she won't buy it.

We'll talk about how to write source notes in the next chapter. Because it's easiest to note which statements or sentences need documenting as you prepare your rough draft, go ahead and read Chapter 8 now.

But that's your only excuse for stopping or delaying your writing! As soon as you've learned the specifics about source notes, sit right down and finish your rough draft. If you keep in mind everything we've talked about in this chapter, writing your draft will be easier than you think.

I promise!

Documenting Your Sources

Y ou must give credit to the source of any facts, expressions or ideas you use in your paper that are not your own. In this chapter, you'll learn the specifics of how to do that.

For many years, the preferred way to credit (or *document*) sources was the *footnote*. Two other forms of documentation—*endnotes* and *parenthetical notes*—are popular now as well. For convenience, I'll refer to all of these different forms collectively as "source notes."

Different strokes for different folks

In an earlier chapter, we discussed the fact that different authorities have set out different rules for bibliography listings. The same is true for source notes. Ask your instructor whose rules you are to follow.

If your teacher doesn't have a preference, you can use the method that seems easiest to you. But use the same method consistently throughout your paper—don't use a footnote on one page, an endnote on another.

Again, I'm going to give you the Modern Language Association of America (MLA) rules. And again, I'll give you the rules for three basic types of materials: a book, magazine article and newspaper article. You can consult the *MLA Handbook* or other reference book if you want specific examples of how to prepare notes for more complicated types of material.

A reminder: What needs documentation

You need a source note when you put any of the following in your paper:

- Quotations taken from a published source
- Someone else's theories or ideas
- Someone else's sentences, phrases or special expressions
- Facts, figures and research data compiled by someone else
- Graphs, pictures and charts designed by someone else

There are some exceptions: You don't need to document the source of a fact, theory or expression that is common knowledge. And you don't need a source note when you use a phrase or expression for which there is no known author.

For example, if you mention that Paris is the capital of France, you don't need to document the source of that information. Ditto for time-worn phrases as "When in Rome, do as the Romans do."

For a test of whether a statement needs a source note, ask yourself whether readers would otherwise think that you had come up with the information or idea all by yourself. If the answer is "yes," you need a source note. If you're in doubt, include a source note anyway.

Footnotes

A footnote is a source note that appears at the "foot" (bottom) of a page of text. The footnote system works like this: You put a raised (superscript) number at the end of the statement or fact you need to document. This serves as a "flag" to readers—it tells them to look at the bottom of the page for a note about the source of the data.

In front of that source note, you put the same superscript number as you put next to the statement or fact in your text. This tells the reader which source note applies to which statement or fact of text.

There is no limit to the number of footnotes you may have in your paper. Number each footnote consecutively, starting with the number 1. For every footnote "flag" in your paper, be sure there is a corresponding source note at the bottom of the page.

What goes into a footnote

You put the same information in your footnote as you do in your bibliography listing—with two differences: In a footnote, the author's name is shown in normal order and the exact page number on which the information being documented appeared in the source is cited.

Most of the information for your footnotes will come from your bibliography cards. But you'll have to look at your note cards to get the actual page number from which various facts came. Arrange elements as follows:

1. Name of the author(s), first name first
2. Title of the book or article
3. Publication information—place of publication, name of the publisher, date of publication, etc.
4. The number of the page(s) on which the information appeared in the work

As with bibliography listings, the content of a footnote depends on the type of reference material. For a refresher on the specific information that you need to include and in what order, see the lists in Chapter 10.

Typing your footnotes

The following general rules apply to all footnotes:

- Put footnotes four lines below the last line of text on the page.
- Indent the first line of a footnote five spaces.
- Single-space lines within an individual footnote; double-space between footnotes.
- Always put the superscript (raised) number of the footnote after the punctuation in your text.
- Abbreviate all months except May, June and July.

Punctuation guidelines

There are specific rules of punctuation and style to follow when you write your footnotes.

For a book, type:

1. The number of the note (superscript)
2. Author's first name, middle name or initial (if any), last name (comma)
3. Title of the book (underlined). No period after the title
4. In parentheses—the place of publication (colon); name of the publisher (comma); year of publication
5. The exact page(s) on which the information you're documenting appears (period). Do not write "page" or "pg." or "p."— just the number alone

For a magazine article, type:

1. The number of the note (superscript)
2. Author's first name, middle name or initial (if any), last name (comma)
3. In quotation marks—title of the article (comma)
4. Name of the periodical in which the article appeared (underlined)
5. The day the periodical was published (for a weekly or biweekly periodical); the month; the year (colon)
6. The exact page number(s) from which the information was taken (period)

For a newspaper article, type:

1. The number of the note (superscript)
2. Author's first name, middle name or initial (if any), last name (comma)

3. In quotation marks—title of the article (comma)

4. Name of the newspaper in which the article appeared (underlined

5. Name of the city and town in which the paper is published (if not part of the name of the paper and/or if the paper is not widely known)—enclose in brackets and do *not* underline

6. The day the paper was published; the month; the year (comma)

7. The edition (abbreviate "edition" as "ed.") if there is more than one published per day (colon)

8. The section and exact page from which the information was taken (period)

Remember, if there is other information on your bibliography card—e.g., the name of an editor or series—you need to include it in your footnote. Arrange information in the same order as you would for a bibliography listing. (See chapter 10 for the correct order.)

Second references

The second time you cite a particular reference as a source of information, you use an abbreviated form of the footnote—just the author's last name and the page number on which the information appeared. (See sample footnote #4 below.)

If you have taken information from two different books written by the same author, you need to include the title of the book as well.

If there is no author given for the work, show the title plus the page number.

Sample footnotes

Below is a sample excerpt from a research paper, followed by four sample footnotes—three to show the different styles necessary for various sources (book, magazine article and newspaper article), the fourth to illustrate how to cite a source for the second time:

> Bob Smith was a leader in the history of Smiths in America. He earned $1 million by the time he was 18.[1] He was awarded honorary degrees in law from Harvard and Princeton.[2] At the age of 35, he invented the first successful widget-spinning gadget,[3] which gave manufacturers a new way to produce widgets.
>
> More than a savvy businessman and accomplished scholar, Smith was a devoted family man. A close friend and neighbor, Bill Jones, once said of Smith: "I never met a man who spent so much time attending to the needs of his wife and children."[4]

[1] Karen A. Jones, <u>The Life and Times of Bob Smith</u> (New York: Smith Press, 1989) 24.

[2] Stan Perkins, "The Life and Times of Bob Smith," <u>Smith Magazine</u> 24 Apr. 1989: 22.

[3] Bill Black, "Bob Smith: The New Widget Spinner," <u>New York Times</u> 16 June 1976, late ed.: A12.

[4] Jones 38.

Endnotes

Endnotes are basically the same thing as footnotes. Within the body of your paper, you indicate the existence of a source note in the same manner as for footnotes—with a superscript (raised) number. The only difference is that you put all of the source listings together—on a separate page at the end of the text—instead of at the bottom of each page.

Title the last page of your paper "Notes" and center that title at the top of the page. Leave a one-inch margin on all sides of the paper (top, bottom, left and right).

List source notes consecutively (put source note 1 first, then note 2, etc.). As with your footnotes, indent the first line of each note. Double-space the entire page (both within individual notes and between notes). Follow the same punctuation rules as those given for footnotes.

Parenthetical notes

Parenthetical notes are probably the easiest way to document sources.

In this system, you put a brief source note right in the body of your text, enclosed in parentheses (hence, the name—parenthetical notes).

Generally, your reference includes only the last name of the author and the page number from which the information was taken. For example:

> Bob Smith was a leader in the history of Smiths in America. He earned a million dollars by the time he was 18 (Jones 24).

To find complete details about the source, readers refer to your bibliography. In this case, they would look for a book or article by "Somebody Jones."

Make sure your note includes enough information so your readers will know exactly which source in your bibliography you are citing.

For example, if your bibliography lists two different works, both written by authors with the last name of Jones., you should include the author's first name in your parenthetical note—i.e., (Karen Jones 24.)

If you have two books written by the same author, include the title of the book you are citing. You can use a one-or two-word abbreviation of the title, if you want.: (Jones, Life and Times 24.)

If your source is a one-page article, you don't have to give any page number in your note.

Now or later?

You can incorporate your source notes as you write your rough draft, or you can put them in during a later draft. I suggest you do the following:

1. As you write your rough draft, mark any statement of fact that needs to be documented. Note the number of the source (the number in the upper left-hand corner of your note card) and the page number from which the material was taken. For example: "Bob Smith was awarded honorary degrees from Harvard and Princeton. (#2-22)."

2. As you prepare your final draft, simply convert these "preliminary" notes into your formal ones.

3. Continue on through the rest of your text, consecutively numbering each note.

4. *If you are using footnotes or endnotes:*
   When you come to the first "preliminary" note in your text, replace the letter and number code with the superscript numeral "1." Find the bibliography card with the same source number as the source number in your preliminary note. Type your footnote or endnote, using the data from the bibliography card. Use the same page number that you show in your "preliminary" note.

5. *If you are using parenthetical notes:*
   Find the bibliography card that matches the source number in your preliminary note. Replace the number-letter code with your parenthetical note. Again, you already know which page number to cite, since you had that information in your preliminary note.

   (Of course, if you're working on a computer, this will only work if you print out a hard copy of your rough draft. When you replace your "preliminary" note letter-number code, you'll lose the information about which source and page number you need to cite.)

Take a deep breath. We're almost there!

Chapter 9

Revising Your Masterpiece

You can breathe a big sigh of relief—your rough draft is done!

Now, you need to take that rough-cut diamond and polish it into a sparkling gem.

In the remaining chapters of this book, we'll revise your rough cut—and revise it again—until we arrive at your final draft.

As we've done with other parts of your assignment, we'll break this process into several steps.

In this chapter, we'll work through two of those steps.

First, you'll edit your paper for content and clarity.

Then, we'll work on the finer points—grammar, spelling, sentence construction, etc.

Phase 1: Edit for meaning

As I said, we're not going to handle all your revisions in one pass. At this point, you still don't need to concentrate on grammar, spelling and other technical aspects of your paper. Of course, when you notice flaws in these areas, fix them. But don't get hung up on them right now.

Rather, during *this* phase of the revision process, you should be trying to:

- *Improve* the flow of your paper—from paragraph to paragraph, sentence to sentence;

- *Organize* your thoughts and information better;

- *Clarify* any confusing points;

- *Strengthen* any weak arguments—by explaining your argument better or adding more data to support your point of view.

Revision checklist

As you review your rough draft, ask yourself the following questions:

- Do your thoughts move logically from one point to the next?

- Is the meaning of every sentence and paragraph crystal clear?

- Does every sentence make a point—or support one?

- Do you move smoothly from one paragraph to the next? Or do you jump randomly from one topic to another?

- Do you support your conclusions with solid evidence—research data, examples, statistics, etc.?

- Do you include a good *mix* of evidence—quotes from experts, scientific data, personal experiences, historical examples?

- Do you have a solid introduction and conclusion?

- Did you write in your own words and style? Or have you merely strung together phrases and quotes "borrowed" from other authors?

- Have you explained your subject thoroughly? Or assumed that readers have more knowledge about it than they actually might? (Remember: *You're* familiar with the topic now, but you've spent *weeks* on it. Just because something is now "obvious" to you doesn't mean your readers will know what you're talking about.)

- Have you convinced your readers that your thesis is valid?

Mark any trouble spots with a colored pencil or pen. If you have an idea of how to fix a section, jot it down on your rough draft.

Then, ask a friend or parent to read your paper. Ask them which sections were confusing, which didn't seem to fit in as written. Make notes on your draft about these trouble points.

Now, sit down and begin to rewrite. Focus on all of those problem areas you found. If necessary, add new information. Play with sentences, paragraphs, even entire sections.

If you're working with a computer, this is fairly easy to do. You can flip words, cut and add sentences, or rearrange whole pages with a few keystrokes.

If you're still hunched over a typewriter or scratching along with pen and paper, you can do the same thing, using scissors and tape. Just cut up the pages of your rough draft and tape them together in their new order.

If you can't figure out how to fix a bothersome sentence or paragraph, take a time-out from writing. Think about what it is you're trying to tell the reader—what point are you trying to get across?

Once you get your thoughts straight, the words will usually take care of themselves.

Phase 2: Do the detail work

When you finish editing for content and meaning, print or type out a clean copy of your paper.

It's time to double-check all of your facts for accuracy. And deal with those things I've been telling you to delay: sentence structure, grammar, punctuation, spelling, etc.

Comb through your paper, and check every piece of factual information against your note cards:

- Did you spell names, terms and places correctly?
- When you quoted dates and statistics, did you get your numbers straight?
- Do you have a source note (or preliminary source note) for every fact, expression or idea that is not your own?
- If you quoted material from a source, did you quote that source exactly, word for word, comma for comma? And did you put the material in quotation marks?

Mark any corrections on your new draft. Again, use a colored pen or pencil so you'll easily spot corrections later.

Smooth out the edges

You've already fixed major problem areas in your paper. Now take an even closer look at your sentences and paragraphs. Try to make them smoother, tighter, easier to understand.

- Is there too much fat? Seize every opportunity to make the same point in fewer words.
- Are there places where phrasing or construction is awkward? Try to rearrange the sentence or section so that it has a better flow.
- Did you use descriptive, colorful words? Did you tell your reader "The planes were damaged" or paint a more colorful and creative picture: "The planes were broken-down hulks of rusted metal—bullet-ridden, neglected warbirds that could barely limp down the runway."
- Consult your thesaurus for synonyms that might do a better job than the words you originally chose. But don't get carried away and use words so obscure that the average reader wouldn't know their meaning.
- Have you overused particular words? Constantly relying on the same verb or adjective makes your writing boring. Again, check your thesaurus for other possibilities.

- How do the words *sound?* When you read
  your paper aloud, does it flow like a
  rhythmic piece of music? Or plod along
  like a dirge? Vary the length of your sentences and paragraphs to make your
  writing more exciting.

Again, mark corrections on your draft with a colored
pen or pencil. No need to retype your paper yet—unless it's
gotten so marked up that it's hard to read!

Check your grammar and spelling

All right, here's the part that almost nobody enjoys.
It's time to rid your paper of mistakes in grammar and
spelling.

I know that I've told you all along that your thoughts
are the most important element of your paper. It's true.
But it's also true that glaring mistakes in grammar and
spelling will lead your teacher to believe that you are
either careless or downright ignorant. Neither of which
will bode well for your final grade.

So, get out your dictionary and a reference book on
English usage and grammar. If you don't happen to own
the latter, check one out from the library, or better yet, buy
your own copy. Ask your instructor to recommend a few
good choices.

Scour through your paper, sentence by sentence,
marking corrections with your colored pen or pencil. Fer-
ret out:

- *Misspelled words.* Check every word. Ask
  yourself: "If I had to bet $100 that I spelled
  that word correctly, would I pull out my
  wallet?" No? Then you'd better look it up in
  the dictionary!

- *Incorrect punctuation.* Review the rules regarding placement of commas, quotation marks, periods, etc. Make sure you follow those rules throughout your paper.

- *Incorrect sentence structure.* Look for dangling participles, split infinitives, sentences that end in prepositions and other "no-no's." Again, review the rules about such matters in your reference book.

Phase 3: Prepare the almost-final draft

Retype your paper, making all those corrections you marked as you completed Phase 2. As you prepare this draft of your paper, incorporate the following three steps:

1. Format the paper according to your teacher's instructions—use the specified page length, margins and line spacing. If you haven't been given any instructions in this area, follow these guidelines:

   - Type or print on one side of the paper only.
   - Use 8 1/2" x 11" paper.
   - Leave a one-inch margin all around—top, bottom, right and left.
   - Indent the first word of each paragraph five spaces from the left margin.
   - Double-space all text. (Single-space footnotes, but double space between each.)
   - Number your pages in the upper right-hand corner of the paper, one half-inch from the top.

Think this is an inconsequential step? Don't kid yourself. After all, if you can't follow the simplest directions about things like margins, why should your instructor believe that you've gotten anything else correct?

2. Incorporate your final footnotes, endnotes or parenthetical notes. For specifics on how to do this, refer back to Chapter 8.

3. Give your paper a title, if you haven't already done so. Your title should be as short and sweet as possible, but it should tell readers what they can expect to learn from your paper. Don't get cute or coy—that's for magazine covers (and it's pretty annoying even then).

You may want to have a headline and a subhead—for example, "Women Air Force Service Pilots: The Almost-forgotten Veterans of World War II." If so, separate your subhead from your main head with a colon and two spaces.

Some teachers prefer that you put your title, name, date and class number on a separate title page. Others want this information to appear at the top of the first page of your text. As always, ask your instructor which page format to follow.

Now, give yourself a big pat on the back! The toughest parts of your assignment are all behind you now.

Chapter 10

Your
Final
Bibliography

By the time you've completed the revision process outlined in Chapter 9, your paper should be in very good shape. Give yourself a round of applause!

There's just a little bit left to do now. You need to prepare your final bibliography, which I'll show you how to do in this chapter. Lastly, you'll need to proofread your paper and type your final draft. I'll give you some great tips on proofreading in Chapter 11.

"Works consulted" vs. "works cited"

Your teacher may ask you to do a "Works Consulted" bibliography—a list of all reference materials you reviewed during your research, *even if nothing from them was incorporated in your paper.* Or, you may be asked to do a "Works Cited" bibliography—listing only those materials you mentioned in your footnotes, endnotes or parenthetical notes.

If your teacher does not specify which type of bibliography to include, choose the first. It will be a better indication of the range of research you've done.

There are some very specific technical rules you must follow when preparing your bibliography. These rules are the same whether you are doing a "works consulted" or "works cited" bibliography.

Your bibliography listings contain virtually the same information as a footnote or endnote. But as we've already learned, there are two big variations: 1) The format and punctuation are different, and 2) the page number references are different.

No, I don't know why. Somewhere along the line, people made up these rules. I'm sure there were good reasons for the things they decided. But the reasons behind the rules aren't important. What *is* important is that you follow the rules—like them or not.

Remember, different authorities prefer different rules, so check with your teacher to find out which rules he or she prefers you follow. Because we've been following MLA rules so far, we'll stick with them.

Laying out your bibliography page

Your bibliography should be at the end of your paper, on a separate page or pages:

- One inch from the top of the each page: Center the title "Works Cited" or "Works Consulted," depending upon which type of bibliography you are doing.

- Use the same margins as you did for the rest of your paper—one inch all the way around.
- Treat your bibliography pages as if they are a continuation of the text of your paper and number them accordingly—*don't* start repaginating.
- List materials in alphabetical order, by the author's last name. If no author is given, go by the first word in the title of the work (unless the first word is "A," "An" or "The," in which case go by the second word).
- The first line of each listing should be flush with the left margin. Indent all lines *except* the first five spaces from the left margin.
- Double-space all listings. And double-space between entries.
- Abbreviate all months except May, June and July.

Sort your bibliography cards

You will take all the information for your bibliography from your bibliography cards. Before you begin typing, put your bibliography cards in the correct alphabetical order. Then, just transfer information, card by card, following the style guidelines listed below.

For a bibliography listing for a book, type:

1. The author's last name (comma), first name and middle name or initial (period and skip two spaces)

2. The title of the book, underlined (period and skip two spaces)

3. The place of publication (colon and skip a space), the name of the publisher (comma, skip a space), the year of publication (period)

For a magazine article, type:

1. The author's last name (comma), first name and middle name or initial (period and skip two spaces)

2. The title of the article (in quotation marks, with a period before the ending quotation marks, then skip two spaces). Note: If the name of the article ends with its own punctuation, such as a question mark, don't put in the period

3. The title of the periodical in which the article appeared, underlined

4. The day of publication (if one is given); the month; the year; (colon and space)

5. The page numbers on which the article appeared (period). If the article didn't appear on consecutive pages, just type the number of the first page followed by a plus (+) sign—e.g., 23+

You do not need to include the volume numbers of a magazine, unless it is a scholarly journal. But if in doubt, include it—better too much information than too little.

For a newspaper article, type:

1. The author's last name (comma), first name and middle name or initial (period and skip two spaces)

2. The title of the article (in quotation marks, with a period before the ending quotation marks, then skip two spaces). Note: If the name of the article ends with its own punctuation, such as a question mark, don't put in the period

3. The title of the newspaper in which the article appeared, underlined

4. The day of publication; the month; the year

5. *If the paper publishes more than one daily edition:* Put a comma after the year, then type the edition information (colon and a space), then the page numbers on which the article appeared. Include the section letter or number if applicable—e.g., A8, etc.

6. *If the paper publishes only one daily edition:* Type a *colon* after the year (space), then the section and page numbers on which the article appeared

If the newspaper isn't a nationally published or well-known paper, add the name of the city and state where it is published after the title. Enclose this information in brackets, but don't underline it. Example: Lawrence Times [Lawrence, NJ]

You do not need to include the volume or issue numbers of the newspaper.

Sample bibliography listings

This except from a sample bibliography page includes listings for a book, a magazine article and a magazine article (in that order):

Jones, Karen A. <u>The Life and Times of Bob Smith.</u> New
    York: Smith Press, 1989.

Perkins, Stan. "The Life and Times of Bob Smith." <u>Smith
    Magazine</u> 24 Apr. 1989: 22-28.

Black, Bill. "Bob Smith: The New Widget Spinner." <u>New
    York Times</u> 16 June 1976, late ed.: A12.

Did you get them all?

Check your bibliography against the text of your paper.
Be sure that you have included all the works cited in your
source notes.

Chapter 11

The Finishing Touches

Can you see it? That light at the end of the tunnel? You should—you're 99 percent of the way *through* the research-paper tunnel.

Don't shut down your mental engine just yet, though— there are a couple of tricky turns left to negotiate.

First, you need to proofread your paper. Then, you need to type or print out a perfect copy of your manuscript —and proofread it again.

To be a good proofreader, you need a sharp eye. Unfortunately, your poor eyes are probably pretty tired by now. And you've become so familiar with your paper that it may be difficult for you to see it clearly. You're likely to read phrase by phrase, rather than word by word. And that means that you'll likely skim over some typos and other errors.

Not to worry, though. In this chapter, I'll show you some tricks that will help you overcome these problems and catch all those little bugaboos in your manuscript.

Trick #1: Read your paper aloud

Go to a quiet room, and read your paper aloud. Not in your head—actually speak the words you have written. Sound them out, syllable by syllable. You'll quickly pick up on typos and misspelled words.

Mark any errors that you find with a brightly colored pen or pencil, and circle them. You want to be able to spot them easily and quickly when you type up your final draft.

Trick #2: Work backward

This is another great trick. Read your paper from back to front, starting with the last word on the last page, working backward toward your introduction. This will help you to focus on each individual word, rather than on the meaning of your phrases and sentences.

Trick #3: Use your computer "spell check"

If you're working on a computer that has a "spell-check" program, be sure to use it. But don't rely on it alone! Yes, the computer will pick up misspelled words. But what if you've used the *wrong* word altogether—used "their" when you meant "there?" If you've *spelled* it right, the computer won't pick up your error. (Some new grammar/usage programs will—lucky you if you have one!)

Trick #4: Have someone else read your paper

Ask a parent to read your paper. Or trade papers with a classmate—you read his if he reads yours. Someone who has never seen your paper before is much more likely to catch a mistake than someone who has read it again and again.

Prepare your perfect copy

After you've proofread your paper several times (*at least* three times), type a clean draft. Then proofread it *again,* to make sure you caught every single error. Miss one or two? Type up those pages again, *and proofread again.* Continue until you're sure your paper is error-free.

Get it all together

Be sure to put your final draft on good quality, white typing or computer printer paper. Don't use that erasable typing paper! It smudges easily.

If you've written your paper on a computer, avoid printing your final draft on a low-quality, dot matrix printer. Manuscripts printed on such printers are hard to read—and the last thing you want to do is make it difficult for your teacher to read your paper. (Some instructors do not even accept such printer copy.)

You can also save your paper on a floppy disk, and take the disk to a quick-print shop. Providing you're working on a compatible computer system, the shop can print out your paper on a laser printer, which produces typeset-quality printing.

If you don't have access to a good printer, or if you're just a lousy typist, you may want to have your final draft prepared by a professional typist. Just make sure the one you select can have your paper done in plenty of time to meet your final deadline!

As soon as you complete your final draft, head right for the copy shop. Pay the buck or two it costs to make a copy of your paper. In the event that you lose or damage your original manuscript, you will have a backup copy.

Turn in your assignment

Put your paper in a new manuscript binder or folder, unless your instructor asks you to do otherwise. Then, turn in your paper—on time, of course!

And congratulate yourself!

You have just completed one of the most challenging assignments you will face as a student. You should feel a real sense of accomplishment. Remember, you can use many of the same strategies you learned as we put together your research paper when you prepare essays, oral reports and other school assignments. And the skills you developed during the past few weeks or months will be useful to you long after you've left the classroom behind for good.

So accept my congratulations, and treat yourself to a little celebration.

You took on the dreaded "R"monster.

And you won!

Index

Write Papers